Donated by a Generous Supporter

Yankee Doodle Numbers

A Connecticut Number Book

Written by Elissa D. Grodin and Illustrated by Maureen K. Brookfield

Maureen Brookfield wishes to thank and acknowledge lighthouse photographer Jeremy D'Entremont (www.lighthouse.cc) for the use of his work in her research.

Sleeping Bear Press™
310 North Main Street, Suite 300
Chelsea, MI 48118
www.sleepingbearpress.com

© 2007 Thomson Gale, a part of the Thomson Corporation.

Thomson, Star Logo and Sleeping Bear Press are trademarks and Gale is a registered trademark used herein under license.

Printed and bound in China.

First Edition

10 9 8 7 6 5 4 3 2 1

Library of Congress Cataloging-in-Publication Data

Grodin, Elissa, 1954-
Yankee doodle numbers : a Connecticut number book / written by Elissa Grodin; illustrated by Maureen Brookfield.
p. cm.
Summary: "Using numbers as its backdrop, this book gives a travelogue of the state's historic moments, symbols, landmarks, and famous people. Included are topics such as lighthouses, railway cars, one-room schoolhouses, and geographic areas"—Provided by publisher.
ISBN-13: 978-1-58536-175-5
ISBN-10: 1-58536-175-5
1. Connecticut—Juvenile literature. 2. Counting—Juvenile literature.
I. Brookfield, Maureen K., 1947- II. Title.

F94.3.G765 2007
974.6—dc22   2006026099

To Chuck and Nicky,
whom I can always count on.

ELISSA

For my twin, Sheila, for all her love and support
over the many years we've lived an ocean apart...........hooray for e-mail!

MAUREEN

Schools were **1** room only
  and kids were just like you,
 a great long time ago,
    about a century or two.

1 2 3 4 5 6 7 8 9 10

1 + 1 = 2

When students at the one-room Cooley School in Granby, on Connecticut's northern border, wanted permission to go to the bathroom, they asked, "Can I go to Massachusetts?" Although the outhouse was just a few feet behind the school, it was across the state line in Southwick, Massachusetts.

Around 1800 there was a border dispute between Connecticut and Massachusetts. The result is a 'notch' of several miles along Connecticut's northern border that belongs to Massachusetts. It is called the Southwick Jog.

The Cooley School was built around 1878. It is one of a dozen one-room schools in Granby. There were one-room school-houses all over the state, where students from ages 5 to 18 studied in one sparse classroom. These early schools were called "common schools." Towns were divided into districts, and each district had a one-room school. Henry Barnard (1811-1900) of Hartford became the first Commissioner of Education in the United States.

one

1

Connecticut was one of the original 13 colonies before America became the United States. During the Revolutionary War (1775-1783), Connecticut was the site of skirmishes in Stonington, Danbury, New Haven, and New London.

General George Washington led America's Continental Army. During the bitter cold winter of 1778-9 his northern brigade set up a winter encampment in Redding, under General Israel Putnam's command. Remnants of a few buildings are scattered through the wooded and hilly terrain. The old encampment is now Putnam Memorial State Park. Wandering through the woods and the remains of soldiers' huts, and poking through the artifacts in the Revolutionary War Museum, you get a feeling of what it was like to be a soldier there, hundreds of years ago.

Our state's role during the American Revolution is proudly on display whenever the state song is sung. Supposedly composed in 1755, "Yankee Doodle" was named our official state song in 1978.

two

2

Shivering cold soldiers
in Washington's brigade
huddled in 2 huts,
on the lookout for a raid.

Pangaea is the name of the ancient land-mass that eventually broke up into the continents of the globe. Before England and New England were divided by the Atlantic Ocean, they were attached. For this reason, their physical environments share similarities, such as soil type. Because of it, the English settlers in Connecticut had less trouble adjusting to their new home. This accounted for much of their success as transplants.

Connecticut is naturally divided into three geographic areas: highlands in the eastern part of the state, more rugged and mountainous highlands in the western part of the state, and low-lands, or a central valley, in between. Connecticut's three major rivers are the Connecticut, Housatonic, and Thames. The Connecticut River is the longest river in New England. It originates at a group of lakes on the U.S.-Canadian border, and runs approx. 400 miles to Saybrook, where it empties into Long Island Sound.

three

3

3 magnificent rivers,
forests that abound,
miles of woods and lakes—
Beauty is all around.

Connecticut has a long tradition of strong women and social activists, people like publisher Hannah Bunce Watson (who kept the *Connecticut Courant* newspaper running during the Revolutionary War) and the four Beecher sisters.

Catharine (1800-1878), Mary (1805-1900), Harriet (1811-1896), and Isabella (1822-1907) Beecher were the daughters of Lyman Beecher, a powerful, opinionated minister. They learned to be outspoken and to work hard for their beliefs.

Catharine was an author and a leader in women's education, opening schools for women in Hartford and other cities. Mary taught for a time at Catharine's Hartford school. She also gave music and drawing lessons in New London. Harriet Beecher Stowe wrote the antislavery novel, *Uncle Tom's Cabin*. Legend claims that when President Abraham Lincoln met her, he said, "So you're the little lady who wrote the book that caused this great war." Isabella was active as a suffragist, fighting for equal rights for women. She helped found the Connecticut Woman Suffrage Association.

four
4

4 Connecticut sisters
who used their education
to improve the lives of others
gained our admiration.

On January 9, 1788, Connecticut became the fifth state in the Union, after Delaware, Pennsylvania, New Jersey, and Georgia. Connecticut has earned four nicknames throughout its history. Each nickname teaches us something different about Connecticut's character.

The Constitution State: In 1639 Connecticut adopted a written document called *The Fundamental Orders*. It set out the structure of Connecticut's earliest form of government, and is thought to be the first state constitution.

The Provisions State: Connecticut had a very successful agricultural economy early on. It exported items like grains, dairy products, and fish to the West Indies in exchange for other goods. During the Revolutionary War, Connecticut stopped business and used all its products to feed the American army, becoming its main supplier.

five
5

CONNECTICUT
"The Constitution State"

The Land of Steady Habits: In the early days of America, before it became the United States, it was a group of colonies, settled by people who had come from Europe. Many settlers were trying to transplant the rules and ways of their old cultures in the new land. Churches were competing for control. There was a lot of conflict and turmoil in this new society. Out of all the colonies, Connecticut had the least amount of strife.

The Nutmeg State: This originally unflattering nickname refers to the wooden nutmegs that Connecticut peddlers used to sell to unsuspecting customers along their routes.

An ice age carved the landscape
where settlements could thrive.
This lush and wooded colony
became state number **5**.

Thousands of years before airplanes, trains, or cars were invented, people traveled around the world on water, conducting business and visiting other lands. Lighthouses have been guiding their way throughout history. Before ships had modern navigation instruments, lighthouses warned sailors of shallow water or rocky coastlines.

In the early days keepers looked after lighthouses. (Eventually lighthouses were automated.) Sometimes they lived in the lighthouse, or in the case of Naylor Jones, the second keeper of Stamford Harbor Light, they lived nearby. When the dock and chicken coop at the lighthouse washed away in a storm, Keeper Jones moved onshore and rowed to work. Stratford was a busy port in the eighteenth and nineteenth centuries. Before there was Stratford Point Light, a fire in an iron basket on a pole was used to guide vessels safely into port. Stratford Point once had a female keeper named Amy Buddington. An 1850 inspection log entry mentions that her son had taken over from her as keeper.

six

6

6 lofty lighthouses
protecting ships that stray,
warning them of rocky coasts
and dangers along the way.

7 handsome trout
relaxing in the lake,
away from rushing falls
and the noise that they make.

Connecticut has 62 state parks and forests spread over its eight counties. Kent Falls State Park is in Litchfield County. Its magnificent series of waterfalls cascade down a mountain stream, finally emptying into the Housatonic River. Native Americans used to fish and camp by these falls. Later, in colonial times, water-powered mills were built along the stream.

Connecticut's oldest state park is Sherwood Island in Fairfield County. A group of farmers settled there in the 1600s, when it was called Fox Island. The descendants of Thomas Sherwood, who moved to this area from England, settled on Fox Island in 1787. They ran a mill and farmed on what came to be called "Sherwood's Island."

Many of Connecticut's state parks participate in a project called "Viewpoints." Outdoor exhibits feature reproductions from nineteenth century American Impressionism paintings, making it possible to see what the Connecticut landscape looked like over a hundred years ago.

seven
7

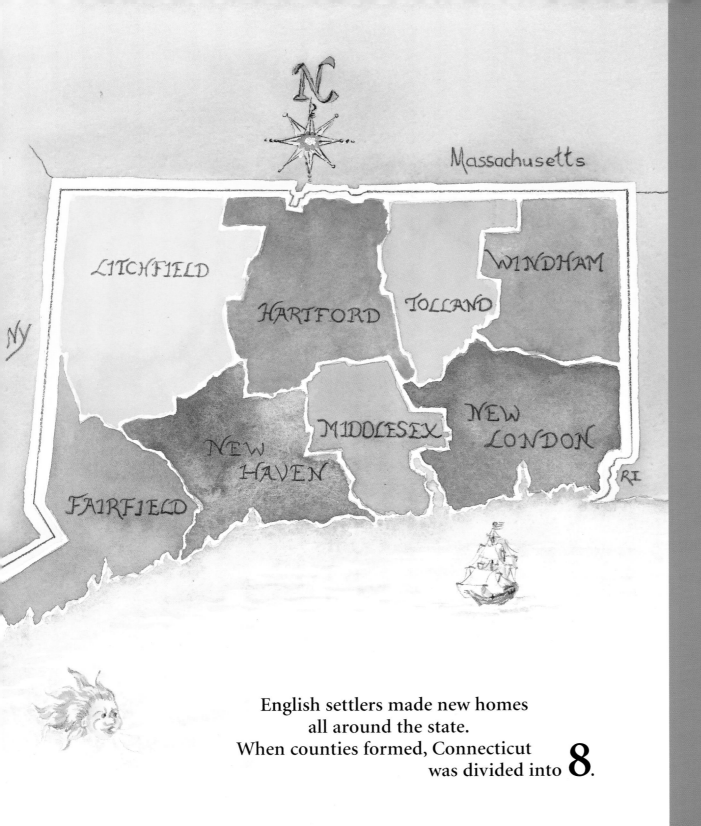

When English settlers came to America, they naturally brought with them many English customs and memories. The system of counties, geographic areas that make up our state, is one example.

In order to keep control over people in the countryside who lived far away from the throne, English kings divided the countryside into districts called 'shires.' That way the king could put one of his people in charge of each shire, and assert his rule over everyone. Although America's system of government is different from England's and does not have a king, the English colonists did divide their new land into districts. The districts were called counties.

Connecticut's eight counties are Fairfield, Hartford, Litchfield, Middlesex, New Haven, New London, Tolland, and Windham. They were founded between 1666 and 1785. Which county do you live in?

eight

8

English settlers made new homes all around the state. When counties formed, Connecticut was divided into **8**.

Railway museums proudly tell the story of our state's rich railroad history, which began in the 1800s. Visitors can see trains over a hundred years old, and even ride on historic streetcars through miles of woods and marshes that look the same as they did a century ago.

"Iron horse" was the nickname given to these great metal machines when people first saw them. Passengers were excited to be able to travel long distances in a short time. There were no cars or buses yet, and the familiar mode of transportation had been horse-drawn carts. But not everyone liked the new trains. Farmers, in particular, didn't like them. The loud noise and smoke from the steam engines scared livestock. If a farm fence in need of repair was down, animals could wander onto the tracks and were sometimes hit by trains.

There are railway museums in five Connecticut counties. The Danbury Union Station, now the Danbury Railway Museum, was used as a location for Alfred Hitchcock's classic thriller, *Strangers on a Train.*

nine

9

9 antique railway cars,
    including an old caboose,
enjoy a peaceful retirement
        instead of being in use.

According to local legend, Jules Bourglay was a young Frenchman who worked in a leather business owned by the Laron family in the 1800s. He was in love with Margaret Laron and hoped to marry her. But Jules made a bad business decision costing the Larons a lot of money, and his hopes were dashed. He disappeared from France and made his way to Connecticut.

Over time Jules became a legendary figure known as the Leatherman. Wearing leather clothing, he hiked ten miles a day for the rest of his life, along a loop between Connecticut and New York. His path was very precise, and the townspeople along his route looked forward to seeing him at regular intervals. It was considered an honor to feed Leatherman, and the shy visitor was loved and offered presents along his way. Leatherman never spoke, but sometimes smiled with appreciation.

In 1885 Chauncey Hotchkiss of Forestville made a map of Leatherman's route, and it was published in the *Hartford Globe*.

ten

10

10 When Leatherman rambled into town on any given day, treats and gifts awaited him from children along the way.

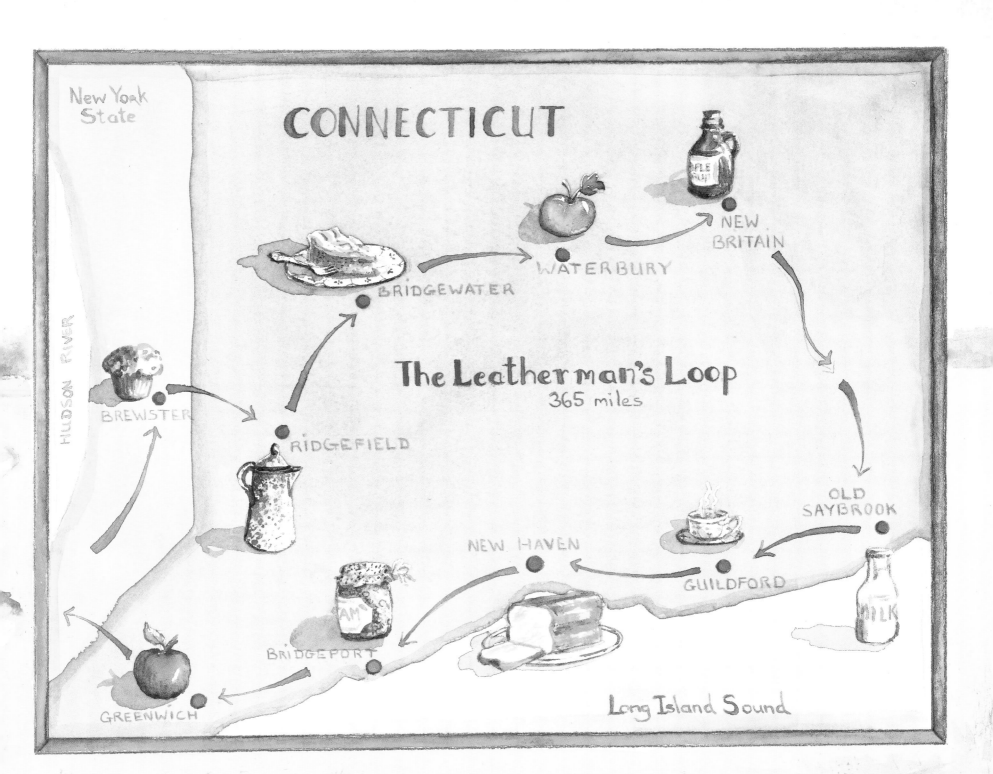

The tradition of candy-making was built on maple sugar. In America's early days candy-making was saved for social occasions. When neighbors gathered together for holidays they would make maple syrup candies and have taffy pulls.

The history of candy-making in New England goes back a long way. An early reference from 1609 tells us: "The Indians get juice from the trees and from it distil a sweet and agreeable liquid." Can you guess what this 'sweet liquid' was?

Popular lore tells us that in the late 1800s George Smith got the idea for what to name candy on a stick when he watched a horse named Lolly Pop run in a race. He and Andrew Bradley were the founders of the Bradley Smith Company in New Haven, manufacturers of candy. In 1931 they patented the name 'lollypop.' Connecticut is also home to Pez candy, which was invented in 1927 in Vienna, Austria. In 1973 an American plant was built in Orange, Connecticut.

eleven
11

11 scrumptious sweets, many would agree, were originally concocted from a humble maple tree.

Growing up in Oxford, Connecticut, Adeline Gray used to jump off the barn roof with an umbrella. She always knew she wanted to be up in the sky, and at the age of 12 Adeline decided to become a parachutist (skydiver). When she was 19 her parents let her take flying lessons, and then there was no stopping her. Adeline learned how to rig parachutes, and during World War II (1939-1945) she became well known for her test-jumps of new parachutes.

Igor Sikorsky (1889-1972) was born in Kiev, in the Ukraine. As a boy he was fascinated by the stories of Jules Verne and the drawings of Leonardo da Vinci. When Igor was 12 he dreamed up a helicopter and built a model of one powered by rubber bands. Igor studied engineering and aerodynamics when he grew up. He dreamed up all sorts of imaginative flying machines, such as flying boats, which he then built. Eventually he built Sikorsky Aviation Corporation in Stratford. In 1939 Igor constructed the first successful helicopter.

twelve
12

Adeline went through 12 umbrellas
before being told to stop.
When jumping off the family barn
she preferred to float than drop.

20 easels all set up
in the beautiful countryside
for 20 fresh air painters,
no longer citified.

The timing couldn't have been better. Just as Florence Griswold was deciding to take in boarders to help pay her bills, a painter named Henry Ward Ranger (1858-1916) was passing through town. In 1899 he decided that Old Lyme was the ideal place to start an artists' colony. Mrs. Griswold's large home made the perfect boardinghouse for Henry and his friends.

Art colonies sprang up across America in the years after the Civil War (1861-1865) and flourished until the 1930s. Art colonies were picturesque places in the countryside where artists lived inexpensively, enjoyed one another's company, learned from each other, and had unlimited subject matter to paint. One of the most successful of these was the Lyme Art Colony, started by Henry Ward Ranger. Over the years, many important painters passed through Mrs. Griswold's house, including Childe Hassam, Willard Metcalf, Matilda Browne, Harry Hoffman, William Chadwick, Charles Gruppe, and others.

twenty

20

Mabel Osgood Wright (1859-1934) grew up in New York City with a love of nature, especially birds. Her first nature essay was published when she was only 16 years old. She moved to Connecticut some years later.

After the National Audubon Society (named after John James Audubon) had disbanded in 1895, Mrs. Wright breathed life back into it by founding the Connecticut Audubon Society in 1898. In 1914 she designed a beautiful bird refuge, the first of its kind. The Birdcraft Museum and Sanctuary in Fairfield is the oldest private bird sanctuary in the U.S. It is now a National Historic Landmark.

The Connecticut Audubon Society operates wildlife sanctuaries all over the state, and preserves thousands of acres of open space for its residents to enjoy.

thirty
30

30 birds in 30 woods
and more along the beach.
Coots and loons and oystercatchers;
hawks and owls that screech.

40 curious scientists
studying the world,
discovering something new
when mysteries are unfurled.

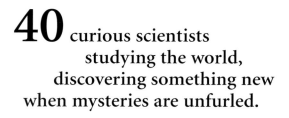

Connecticut has a rich tradition of scientists who study the universe to better understand how it operates. Why do objects fall down instead of up? Why does the needle on a compass point north? There is an area of science to satisfy every curiosity.

Benjamin Silliman (1779-1864), born in Trumbull, was a geologist, chemist, and lawyer. He inspired thousands of students over 50 years of teaching, and helped to found Yale Medical School. In the 1860s New Haven astronomer Edward Herrick (1811-1862) reported in the *American Journal of Science* a sighting of an exceptionally large group of shooting stars in the nighttime sky. This sighting was soon confirmed by stargazers in England. Almira Phelps (1793-1884) of Berlin, Connecticut, wrote textbooks on chemistry, geology, and botany. In 1983 geneticist Barbara McClintock (1902-1992) of Hartford was the first American woman to win an unshared Nobel Prize. The list of Connecticut scientists goes on and on.

The U.S. government started giving out patents to inventors in 1790. From that year until 1841, Connecticut led all states in patents per capita (the most patents for its population size).

A few early inventors were clockmaker Eli Terry (1772-1852); Eli Whitney (1765-1825), inventor of the cotton gin; and rubber manufacturer Charles Goodyear (1800-1860). Less well known is Mary Kies, who invented a method of weaving straw with silk to make hats. She was the first woman to receive a U.S. patent, in 1809.

From 1871 to 1958 the Frisbie Baking Company in Bridgeport sold pies to local colleges. When students started tossing the empty pie tins around, the game of Frisbee was invented.

David N. Mullany of Fairfield invented the Wiffle ball in 1953. He cut holes in a plastic globe in order to make it easier for his son to learn how to throw a curveball.

fifty
50

At Mrs. Frisbie's bakeshop
the pie tins bore her name.
50 students used them
and invented a brand-new game.

60 workers humming along,
using brand-new tools.
The Industrial Revolution came
and changed a lot of rules.

The Industrial Revolution (1790-1860) was a time when machines began to manufacture some of the goods that had traditionally been made by hand. New machines were being invented that gave rise to new industries, and industries gave rise to cities that became crowded with factories and smokestacks.

In 1790 Zadoc Benedict of Danbury became the first hatmaker to move his business from his home into a shop. Other hatmakers followed his example, and the hat industry was born. Soon hat production was so great that Danbury got the nickname "Hat City."

Clocks were another specialty of our state. Seven Connecticut clock companies led the country in manufacturing clocks after the Industrial Revolution. The American Clock & Watch Museum in Bristol displays over 1,500 clocks, and houses a permanent exhibit called "Connecticut Clockmaking and the Industrial Revolution."

sixty
60

Starting in 1929 the Great Depression was a time when businesses and industries slumped. The country's economy was very bad; many people lost their jobs and struggled to earn a living. This lasted until the beginning of the 1940s.

On May 6, 1935, President Franklin Delano Roosevelt (1882-1945) formed the Works Progress (later Work Projects) Administration (WPA). The WPA created jobs for unemployed people in towns and cities across the country. These workers were commissioned to build new schools and other municipal buildings. President Roosevelt gave hundreds of out-of-work artists jobs, painting large murals in these new buildings.

Many of these gorgeous murals have been destroyed, but Connecticut understood the historic importance of these magnificent artworks. Perhaps the biggest collection of WPA murals in the U.S. is in Norwalk.

seventy
70

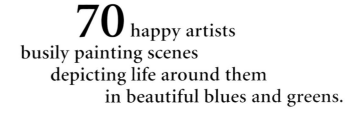

70 happy artists
busily painting scenes
depicting life around them
in beautiful blues and greens.

80 The British fleet supplied the war
but Connecticut got a notion.
privateers fought back
and prevailed out on the ocean.

If you owned a ship during the American Revolution, you could join in the fight against England.

Privateers were privately owned ships, armed and licensed to attack and capture enemy merchant ships. Millions of dollars worth of British supplies were regularly stolen by privateers and given instead to American soldiers. The privateers were allowed to keep half of the profit from each "prize."

One of the most successful privateering ships was Nathaniel Shaw's *American Revenue*, which sailed from 1777 to 1779 and hailed from New London, the state's leading base for privateers. Two hundred to three hundred other Connecticut privateers sailed from New Haven, Wethersfield, Hartford, and Saybrook, capturing nearly 500 English vessels over the course of the war.

eighty
80

Since 1673 the Boston Post Road (U.S. Highway 1) served as the main roadway connecting New York City to New England. In the 1920s another roadway was proposed in order to reduce congestion. The Merritt Parkway, running 37 miles on Rte. 15 in Fairfield County, finally opened on June 30, 1938.

More than just an ordinary roadway, the Merritt Parkway is considered a work of art for the way it combines engineering, landscaping, architecture, and sculpture. It was designed to emphasize the beauty of the landscape. When it first opened people used it as a park because it was so beautiful and restful. Regulations about picnicking had to be enforced right away.

Connecticut Highway Department architect George Dunkelberger came up with a unique, delightful design for each of the roadway's 68 original bridges. Two thousand Depression-era unemployed workers were hired to build the bridges as part of the WPA.

ninety
90

90 cars on a roadway
green as any park,
a serpentine of taillights
traveling in the dark.

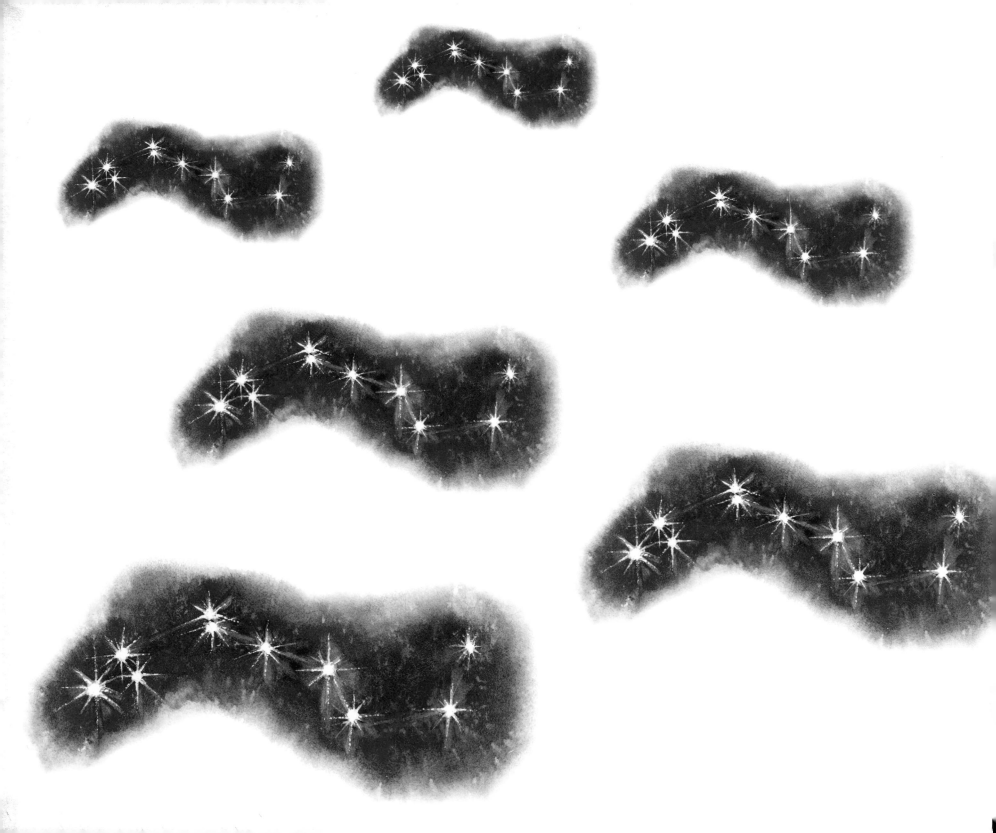

100 distant stars—
Each could be a sun
with planets of its own.
Are we the only one?

Human beings love to look at the stars. The first constellations were picked out of the sky and given names around 5,000 years ago by the Babylonians. The nearest star to Earth is the sun.

Maps showing the starry sky have been around for thousands of years, but planets have been much harder to plot on a map. Planets change their positions all the time because they orbit in relation to each other. Machines that could accurately show the positions of planets came along in the 1920s. They were called planetariums. Planetariums are like time machines; they can project how the nighttime sky would look from Earth thousands of years in the past or the future.

There are planetariums and observatories all over Connecticut where you can learn about things like black holes, blue giants, and why stars twinkle but planets don't. Built in 1954, the University of Connecticut Planetarium in Storrs is the oldest in the state. Where is the one nearest to you?

one
hundred
100

Elissa D. Grodin

Elissa Grodin attended Dartmouth College and the School of Visual Arts. She has written for the *Times Literary Supplement* and *New Statesman*. *Yankee Doodle Numbers* is her fifth book with Sleeping Bear Press. She also wrote *N is for Nutmeg: A Connecticut Alphabet*; *D is for Democracy: A Citizen's Alphabet*; *Everyone Counts: A Citizen's Number Book*; and the recent retelling of Oscar Wilde's classic story *The Happy Prince*. Elissa lives in Wilton, Connecticut.

Maureen K. Brookfield

Maureen Brookfield is an accomplished realistic artist best known for her watercolor paintings. She lived and studied in the New York/New Jersey area for many years, attending the Parsons School of Design and the Art Center of Northern New Jersey and studying with several prominent and nationally known artists. Her works have won many awards and been widely exhibited, including such prestigious shows as the New England Watercolor Society and the Commonwealth Museum in Boston. Her paintings can be found in both national and international corporate and private collections. Maureen now lives with her husband, Don, in Marshfield, Massachusetts, and is very active in local and regional art associations. She also illustrated *N is for Nutmeg: A Connecticut Alphabet*; *E is for Empire: A New York State Alphabet*; and *Times Square: A New York State Number Book* from Sleeping Bear Press.